# CLASSIC ANTHEMS

## for mixed-voice choirs

NOVELLO

Published by
**Novello Publishing Limited**
14-15 Berners Street,
London W1T 3LJ, UK.

Exclusive Distributors:
**Music Sales Limited**
Distribution Centre, Newmarket Road,
Bury St Edmunds, Suffolk IP33 3YB, UK.

**Music Sales Corporation**
180 Madison Avenue, 24th Floor,
New York NY 10016, USA.

**Music Sales Pty Limited**
Units 3-4, 17 Willfox Street, Condell Park
NSW 2200, Australia.

Order No. NOV294371
ISBN 978-1-78305-413-8

Music processed by Paul Ewers Music Design.
Project Manager and Editor: Jonathan Wikeley.
Introductory notes by Thomas Lydon, Matthew O'Donovan and Jonathan Wikeley.

Printed in the EU.

www.musicsalesclassical.com

# Contents

# O holy night!
## Adolphe Adam (1803-1856)

This enduring carol, originally written for solo voice with accompaniment, is but a footnote to the career of one of France's great men of the theatre.

Possessed of a bottomless compositional fluency and a Rossinian appetite for fine living, Adam was a popular fixture in early 19th-century Paris. He wrote more than 80 works for the stage, the tunes from which were whistled in streets by folk whose children would later whistle the arias of Offenbach. Few are regularly performed, but his ballet *Giselle* has been danced by Pavlova, Nijinsky and most of the greats since.

The first Christmas performances of this song would have coincided with the first season of Adam's ill-fated attempt to open a third opera house in Paris, the Opéra-National. Written in a period of feverous uncertainly for the composer – against the backdrop of political unrest, industrial ferment and cholera – the soaring clarity of the melody has inspired arrangers and performers of every succeeding generation.

# Come, Holy Ghost
## Thomas Attwood (1765-1838)

Thomas Attwood is perhaps best known as the composer of such charming miniatures as *Come Holy Ghost*, which is in essence a simple, three-verse hymn. Its elegant melody, first sung by soprano, then by a chorus (or quartet and chorus) is reminiscent of Mozart's delicate masterpiece, *Ave verum corpus*.

This is perhaps unsurprising – Attwood took composition lessons from Mozart in Vienna, and one of his contemporaries quotes Mozart as saying: 'He partakes more of my style than any scholar I ever had; and I predict, that he will prove a sound musician.' Attwood worked closely with the royal family throughout his life. He taught music to the Prince of Wales, was appointed composer and eventually organist to the Chapel Royal, and organist at St Paul's Cathedral (he is buried under the organ there). He wrote the anthem *I was glad* for the coronation of King George IV.

# And I saw a new heaven
## Edgar Bainton (1880-1956)

This anthem was completed in June 1928, during Bainton's second period on the staff at the Newcastle upon Tyne Conservatory of Music.

The composer, who is perhaps in retrospect most celebrated in the city of Sydney, Australia, where he was to later settle, had already seen much of life. An ill-timed musical pilgrimage to Bayreuth saw him interned at Ruhleben for the duration of the First World War. He was put in charge of the music and, amid the hardship, it was a creative period for him. In early 1918 his health declined and he was sent to The Hague to convalesce. He soon made his musical mark there, and following the Armistice he became the first Englishman to conduct the Amsterdam Concertgebouw Orchestra.

Another figure known largely these days only for the work present here, Bainton saw considerable success in Australia with his opera *The Pearl Tree*, and his choral works and partsongs were frequently performed in this country during his lifetime.

# Save us, O Lord
## Edward Bairstow (1874-1946)

A Yorkshireman who, following studies at Balliol College, Oxford and Westminster Abbey, returned to the north for good, Bairstow worked as organist at Wigan Parish Church, Leeds Parish Church and – accepting a pay cut from the latter position – York Minster.

He became a prominent figure in the inter-war period, and his strident opinions on the music industry and the beginnings of the recording industry were debated across the country.

He was appointed professor of music at Durham University in 1929 and received a knighthood in 1932.

His outspoken adjudication was much celebrated at Yorkshire festivals, particularly his assertion, attested by Francis Jackson, that 'when God gave man a tenor voice he took away his brains'.

# How lovely are thy dwellings
## Johannes Brahms (1833-1897)

*How lovely are thy dwellings* is the fourth movement from Brahms's *Ein deutches Requiem*, written between 1865-1868. The composer's great friend Joachim held that the work was written in memory of his recently deceased mother, while others have pointed to the death of his mentor Schumann in 1865. In any case the work is not a Requiem in the strict liturgical sense (indeed its content is more by way of spiritual encouragement to the living than prayer for the dead) but rather a setting in seven movements of assorted passages from Luther's German translation of the scriptures. The first performance of the complete Requiem was given in Leipzig in 1869, and its first performance in English took place in London just two years later, in 1871.

The fourth movement has a long history as a standalone English anthem, and its publication in this form 100 years ago by Novello ensured its cherished place in the repertoire of countless church, collegiate and cathedral choirs to this day. Though the 1911 edition has been reprinted numerous times in the intervening years, the anthem has never appeared with an accompaniment appropriate for performance on the organ, in spite of the fact that the majority of the anthem's performances over the years must have used the instrument. At its best, the piano accompaniment fails to make effective use of the organ's potential to realise the original orchestral colours, and at its worst it is unplayable on the instrument without significant alteration.

This new organ accompaniment has been prepared from Brahms's full score with a view to providing organists with a version that is both comfortably playable on the instrument and truer to the orchestral colours of the original. Indeed, the organ is particularly well suited to conveying the textural subtleties of this movement – the lyrical woodwind passages in particular. The given registrations are suggestions for guidance and need not be followed exactly; indeed, although three manuals are indicated, the accompaniment can easily be performed on two or even (with minimal adaptation) one. It may be helpful to note that passages marked to be played on the Choir are usually those where the melody is doubled at the octave with the flutes in the original score; the use of 4' flute tone is recommended in such places. (Note, however, that the RH octave doubling which will be familiar to users of the 1911 piano reduction is not recommended as an alternative, as it tends to create a rather shriller effect when played on the organ than is called for by the score.) Organs vary widely as to the balance between different divisions; it is left to the organist's discretion as to whether to couple the Swell in such passages. If the divisions are not coupled, then the small LH notes in bb. 3-4 and 88-89 should be played. Another area in which organists may wish to exercise discretion is the means by which the $\boldsymbol{fp}$ markings in bb. 66-69 and 74-77 are realised. While on some instruments the effect may be effectively obtained by the use of the Swell box, on others the organist may wish to play the passages in question on the Swell, jumping down to the Great for each accented quaver – or alternatively playing the LH part of the relevant bars on the Great, doubling each accented RH chord with the LH.

## Ave verum corpus
### Edward Elgar (1857-1934)

Elgar knew a good tune when he had composed one, and this *Ave verum corpus*, published in 1902 as Op. 2 no. 1, is an adaptation of a *Pie Jesu* setting he wrote in 1887. He had by this time ceased to write Catholic liturgical music and with the Enigma Variations and *The Dream of Gerontius* under his belt, was lauded across Europe. However, even at his most characteristically self-dismissive, Elgar could not hide his affection for this diatonic miniature, writing in a letter to August Jaeger, his friend and publisher at Novello: 'I send you the *Ave verum* again... the Music is too sugary I think but it is nice & harmless & quite easy'.

## Evening Hymn
### Henry Balfour Gardiner (1877-1950)

Henry Balfour Gardiner is a somewhat shadowy figure in the generation that bridged the Victorians and the post-war greats. A worldly musician, who studied at length in Frankfurt, he, like his contemporaries Vaughan Williams and Holst, collected folk songs, using the material in new forms – from solo songs to the very largest instrumental forces.

Much of his output is lost or unpublished, and his greatest contribution to posterity was behind the scenes, in providing monetary assistance (he had private wealth) and performance opportunities to his peers.

It is perhaps fitting that this most self-critical of artists is remembered for his heart-felt setting of the Latin compline hymn *Te lucis ante terminum*, a plea to a higher power for protection at the close of the day.

## My beloved spake
### Patrick Hadley (1899-1973)

Hadley, a composer who followed in Stanford's footsteps on the staff at the Royal College of Music and at Cambridge Unviersity; who studied with Wood and Vaughan Williams; and who was the inter-war go-to man for advice among the musical elite, wrote regrettably little of the stuff. He was a master of pastoral nostalgia, and this setting of the Song of Solomon, a firm liturgical favourite, gives a glimpse of a lyric, post-Vaughan Williams sound world which can be more fully explored in his songs and large-scale works

# 'Hallelujah' Chorus
## George Frideric Handel (1685-1759)

The 'Hallelujah' chorus, arguably the most famous choral work of the western classical tradition, is the closing number of the second part of Handel's *Messiah*.

Such is the strength of Handel's word setting that this emphatic, triumphal paean retains its appeal in spite of the cultural overexposure and controversy to which it has been subjected, remaining a firm favourite with choirs and arrangers alike.

The first performance of Messiah was given in Dublin in 1742 as the high point of a full season of Handel's work. It was a charity event, held in aid of local causes, and in order to get the maximum attendance in Neale's new music hall in Fishamble Street, the men were asked to remove their swords, and the ladies the hoops in their dresses.

The tradition of standing during performances of the 'Hallelujah' chorus, still indulged at some performances in Britain, is said to have been started by King George II at the work's opening run in London in 1743.

# Bring us, O Lord God
## William Harris (1883-1973)

Harris's *Bring us, O Lord God* and its sister work *Faire is the heaven* are two of the most rewarding anthems for double choir in the Anglican canon. This piece was composed in 1959, not long before Harris's retirement from a distinguished career as a teacher and director of music.

A renowned choir trainer, the idiomatic part writing and textural mastery that Harris achieves in the work are testament to his tireless efforts at the musical helm of institutions such as New College, Oxford; Christ Church Cathedral; and St George's Chapel, Windsor.

# The heavens are telling
## Franz Josef Haydn (1732-1809)

Written between 1796 and 1798, Haydn's *Creation* met with immediate popularity, and has been considered by many throughout its history to be his masterpiece. Like all English oratorios in the late 18th century, *Creation* was concert-hall or theatre fare; performances in church buildings did not begin to take place until several decades later. 'The heavens are telling', the closing movement of part one, is with little doubt the work's best-known chorus.

The eccentricity of the text is due to its rather circuitous origins. The work had its genesis in an English libretto handed to Haydn (having been previously rejected by Handel) by J. P. Salomon at the end of his visit to England in 1794-5. On returning home, Haydn – not an English-speaker – handed it to Baron van Swieten, who produced a German translation for Haydn to compose from, before awkwardly re-translating it back into English to fit Haydn's music. While van Swieten's English version is now too much cherished to be done away with, performers wishing to sing a more lucid and meaningful text may wish to consider the following two amendments:

1.  'The wonder of his work displays the firmament' can be rendered coherently with a simple reordering of the words: 'the firmament displays the wonder of his work'.

2.  'To day that is coming speaks it the day; the night that is gone, to following night' makes more sense in the version of 1832 by Haydn's pupil, Sigismond Neukomm: 'How day unto day is speaking his praise; while night unto night his glory proclaims.'

For many decades organists have made do with Vincent Novello's keyboard reduction, in many ways not well suited to the instrument, and lacking some important textural detail. In preparing the new organ accompaniment, the aim has therefore been to preserve both the grandeur and contrapuntal clarity of Haydn's orchestral score, while using the instrument's resources to the best advantage. Certain passages have presented challenges in this regard and are worthy of comment. The repeated RH quavers in bars 154-158 and from 175 onwards are preferred to any alternative, they may prove difficult to play on organs with a very heavy key action. In this case, an alternative figuration such as the following may be employed:

Likewise, the pedal *glissandi* in bars 182 and 184 may be impractical on some pedalboards. If required, they can be taken by the left hand, and the LH crotchet rest transferred to the pedal part. Organists have often been tempted to simplify the textures in this piece and minimise the use of the pedals, taking most of the bass line with the left hand. While this seems an attractive proposition and would not necessarily be wrong in a small-scale performance (we know that Haydn used a smaller orchestra in private court performances), to do so hardly does justice to Haydn's published score, which calls upon a weighty orchestra including contrabassoon and trombones, and in places provides for independent cello and bass parts. In other words, 16' bass tone is essential. At the first public performance the orchestra numbered about 120, double the size of the choir.

# Vox dicentis: clama
## Edward Naylor (1867-1934)

Edward Woodall Naylor, son of composer John Naylor and father of composer Bernard Naylor studied at Cambridge University and under Stanford at the Royal College of Music. He held posts at St Michael's, Chester Square and St Mary's, Kilburn in London before returning to Cambridge as organist at Emmanuel College, later becoming lecturer.

The range of textures in this piece reflect his eclectic influences; like his father, he was clearly influenced by various musical styles, reaching back to the renaissance, although he never copied his father's liturgical use of the bagpipes.

Naylor's best work is vocal, and his opera *The Angelus*, produced at Covent Garden in 1909, won the Ricordi prize for English Opera

# Hear my prayer, O Lord
## Henry Purcell (1659-1695)

This setting of the opening to Psalm 102 was composed in the early 1680s. Purcell, who was in his early twenties, had succeeded John Blow as organist of Westminster Abbey around the beginning of the decade and his star was in the ascendant as a court composer.

In this piece he pulls off a remarkable compositional coup: a single, gradual climax, lasting over two minutes and culminating on the final repetition of the word 'come', is achieved through a sublime, freely developing eight-part weave of the opening material. The remarkable harmonies that result from the chromatic inflections on the word 'crying' all serve the mounting tension in this extraordinary miniature.

Study of the autograph manuscript suggests that the anthem was intended to be the opening part of a larger work that was never completed.

# Remember not, Lord, our offences
## Henry Purcell (1659-1695)

One of Purcell's rare full anthems, *Remember not, Lord, our offences* sets text from the Order for the Visitation of the Sick and was composed between 1679–81, around the time of his early career at the musical helm of Westminster Abbey.

# Thou knowest, Lord, the secrets of our hearts
## Henry Purcell (1659-1695)

This simple yet powerful homophonic work was written as part of Purcell's music for the state funeral of Queen Mary II in 1695. It is the second setting that Purcell made of this text from the Anglican burial service, and was sung at Purcell's own funeral that same year.

# Rejoice in the Lord alway
## George Rathbone (1874-1951)

Manchester-born pianist and organist George Rathbone made a name for himself on both sides of the Atlantic in the inter-war years with his secular songs and large-scale vocal works. Of all his religious music, including several tuneful anthems and a set of Evening Canticles in B flat, this memorable anthem has endured in popularity, appearing in concerts and services across Europe and the USA.

# I saw the Lord
## John Stainer (1840-1901)

The emotive word setting that characterises Stainer's output is seen at its best in this extended anthem. A first-class organist, a scholar and educationist, who is credited with revitalising the worship at St Paul's Cathedral, he was a prolific liturgical composer, with a handful of cantatas (including the ubiquitous *Crucifixion*), two dozen services, more than 150 hymn tunes, and just shy of 50 anthems under his belt. The populist appeal of his music and the liturgical utility of his texts has made a small number of his works, including this one, enduring favourites.

# Ascribe unto the Lord
## Samuel Sebastian Wesley (1810-1876)

Samuel Sebastian Wesley forged new ground for English worship music with a fusion of old and new musical styles. He was most successful in this regard with his extended anthems, in which he indulged in equal measure his facility with traditional counterpoint and more modern styles of melody and recitative.

No finer example of his craft is there than his mature anthem *Ascribe unto the Lord*. It was written in 1851, by which time Wesley was able to channel his influences freely to serve his very personal harmonic and dramatic impulses.

This edition has been prepared using both the original Novello edition with organ accompaniment and the autograph orchestral score, prepared for the 1865 Three Choirs Festival in Gloucester.

The old Novello edition was at times unclear as to pedalling in the organ part, something that this edition has attempted to clarify. Certain pedal passages provide challenges to the organist; the passage from the second quaver of bar 157 to the first crotchet of bar 159 may be taken by the left hand if the manuals use 16' tone.

The instruction 'Full organ' is somewhat ambiguous, but is most likely to mean 'Full Great': a chorus of diapasons up to sesquialtera and mixtures, plus trumpet – a clear, bright sound, but not an overly strident one, and with no heavy pressure reeds. The Swell was short compass, and was unlikely to have been coupled, and the gentle Choir division would not have made much of an impact.

## Blessed be the God and Father
### Samuel Sebastian Wesley (1810-1876)

Despite having a reasonable claim to being the best thing to happen to English music since Henry Purcell, Samuel Sebastian Wesley cut a jagged path through the music establishment.

The grandson of Methodist leader Charles Wesley and son of composer Samuel Wesley, Samuel Sebastian, whose middle name derived from his father's love of Bach, tempered musical endeavour with administrative friction (he was notoriously difficult to work with) in the cathedrals of Hereford, Exeter, Winchester and Gloucester, and Leeds Parish Church.

*Blessed be the God and Father* is an early work, written in Hereford for an Easter Day service. From curious beginnings – the first performance was given by a row of trebles and a single bass because all the other adult members of the choir were in holy orders and held livings elsewhere – this work now receives particular affection from Anglican musicians. It was performed by the choir of Westminster Abbey at Queen Elizabeth II's wedding to Prince Philip.

# O holy night!

*'Noël'*

J. S. Dwight

Adolphe Adam
arr. John E. West

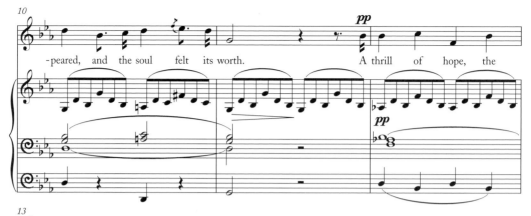

-peared, and the soul felt its worth. A thrill of hope, the

wea - ry world re - joic - es, For yon - der breaks a new and glo - rious morn!

SOLO

Fall on your knees! Oh, hear the an - gel

CHORUS SOPRANO *pp sotto voce*

Fall on your knees! Oh,

ALTO *pp sotto voce*

Fall on your knees! Oh,

TENOR *pp sotto voce*

Fall on your knees! Oh,

BASS *pp sotto voce*

Fall on your knees! Oh,

add to Ch. & Sw.

6

SOPRANO (or TENOR) SOLO

Led by the light of faith se-rene-ly beam - ing, With glow-ing

hearts by His cra - dle we stand; So led by

light of a star sweet-ly gleam - ing, Here came the wise men__ from the O - rient

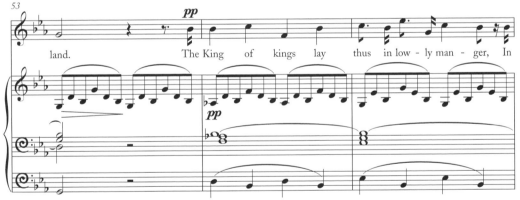

land. The King of kings lay thus in low - ly man - ger, In

*pp*

*pp*

all our tri - als born to be our friend;__ He knows our

*add to Ch. & Sw.*

*f*

*mp*

# Come, Holy Ghost

Hymn for Whitsuntide

Thomas Attwood

**VOICES ALONE**

SOPRANO

En - a - ble__ with per - pet - ual light The dull - ness

ALTO

En - a - ble with per - pet - ual light The dull - ness

TENOR

En - a - ble with per - pet - ual light The dull - ness

BASS

En - a - ble with per - pet - ual light The dull - ness

14

One; That through the a - ges all a - long This may be our

One; That through the a - ges all a - long This may be our

One; That through the a - ges all a - long This may be our

One; That through the a - ges all a - long This may be our

end - less song, Praise to Thy e - ter - nal mer - it, Fa - ther,

end - less song, Praise to Thy e - ter - nal mer - it, Fa - ther,

end - less song, Praise to Thy e - ter - nal mer - it, Fa - ther,

end - less song, Praise to Thy e - ter - nal mer - it, Fa - ther,

# And I saw a new heaven

Revelations 21: 1-4

Edgar L. Bainton

bride a-dorn-ed for her hus - band.

bride a-dorn-ed for her hus - band.

-par - ed as a bride a-dorn-ed for her hus - band.

-par - ed as a bride a-dorn-ed for her hus - band.

And I heard a great voice out of heaven, say-ing,

Be- hold, the tab - er-na-cle of God is with men, and he will dwell with them and

Be- hold, the tab-er - na-cle of God is with men, and he will dwell with them and

Be- hold, the tab - er-na-cle of God is with men, and he will dwell with them and

Be- hold, the tab - er - na-cle of God is with men, and he will dwell with them and

they shall be his peo- ple, and God him-self___ shall be with them and be___ their

they shall be his peo- ple, and God him-self___ shall be with them and be___ their

they shall be his peo- ple, and God him-self___ shall be with them and be___ their

they shall be his peo- ple, and God him-self___ shall be with them and be___ their

*Composed for the Festival of Wigan and District Church Association, November 1902*

# Save us, O Lord

Edward C. Bairstow

Antiphon from the
Office of Compline

# How lovely are thy dwellings

from *A German Requiem*

Psalm 84: 1, 2 & 4

Johannes Brahms
Organ part arr.
Matthew O'Donovan

*\* see introduction*

+Gt. to Ped.

+Gt. to Ped.

# Ave verum corpus

Fourteenth-century hymn

Edward Elgar
Op. 2 no. 1

**SOPRANO** *cresc.* 18

Cu - ius la - tus per - fo - ra - tum ve - ro flu - xit san - gui -

*cresc.*

*senza Ped.*

21 *f* *p*

- ne: es - to no - bis præ - gu - sta - tum, mor - tis in ex - a - mi - ne.

*f* *dim.*

*pp* 26 *cresc.* *f*

Cu - ius la - tus per - fo - ra - tum ve - ro flu - xit san - gui - ne: es - to

*pp* *cresc.* *f*

Cu - ius la - tus per - fo - ra - tum ve - ro flu - xit san - gui - ne: es - to

*pp* *cresc.* *f*

Cu - ius la - tus per - fo - ra - tum ve - ro flu - xit san - gui - ne: es - to

*pp* *cresc.* *f*

Cu - ius la - tus per - fo - ra - tum ve - ro flu - xit san - gui - ne: es - to

*pp* *cresc.* *f*

*Ped.*

no-bis præ-gu-sta-tum, mor-tis in ex-a-mi-ne._____ O

no-bis præ-gu-sta-tum, mor-tis in ex-a-mi - ne._____

no-bis præ-gu-sta-tum, mor-tis in ex-a-mi - ne._____ O

no-bis præ-gu- sta-tum, mor-tis in ex-a-mi - ne._____

cle - mens, O dul-cis Je-su, fi-li Ma-ri - æ._____

O pi - e, O dul-cis Je-su, fi-li Ma-ri - æ, Ma-ri - æ.

cle - mens, O dul-cis Je-su, fi-li Ma-ri - æ, Ma-ri - æ.

O pi - e, O dul-cis Je-su, fi-li Ma-ri - æ, Ma-ri - æ.

# Evening Hymn

early Latin hymn

Henry Balfour Gardiner

* Soft reed. 4', 8', 16'.

\* Between the signs ⊦ the voices are to sing unaccompanied: the organ part is only added for the purposes of practice.

ny: De - fend_____ us from un - chas - ti - ty.
-me Ne pol - lu - an - tur cor - po - ra.

ny: De - fend_____ us from un - chas - ti - ty.
-me Ne pol - lu - an - tur cor - po - ra.

ny: De - fend_____ us from un - chas - ti - ty.
-me Ne pol - lu - an - tur cor - po - ra.

ny: De - fend_____ us from un - chas - ti - ty.
-me Ne pol - lu - an - tur cor - po - ra.

# My beloved spake

Song of Solomon 2:10-13

Patrick Hadley

64

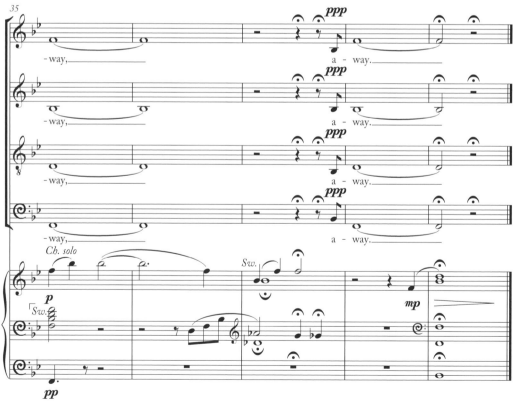

# 'Hallelujah' Chorus

### from *Messiah*

Revelation 19:6, 11:15, 19:16

George Frideric Handel

70

* Handel himself wrote both notes.

LORDS, KING OF KINGS, AND LORD OF LORDS, and

LORDS, KING OF KINGS, AND LORD OF__ LORDS, and

LORDS, KING OF KINGS, AND LORD OF__ LORDS, and

LORDS, KING OF KINGS, AND LORD OF LORDS, and he shall

he shall reign for ev-er and ev - er, KING OF

he shall reign for ev - er and ev - er, for ev-er and

he shall reign for ev - er and ev - er, for ev-er and

reign for ev - er, for ev-er and ev - er, for ev-er and

*Trumpets*

*Strings*

# Bring us, O Lord God

John Donne

William H. Harris

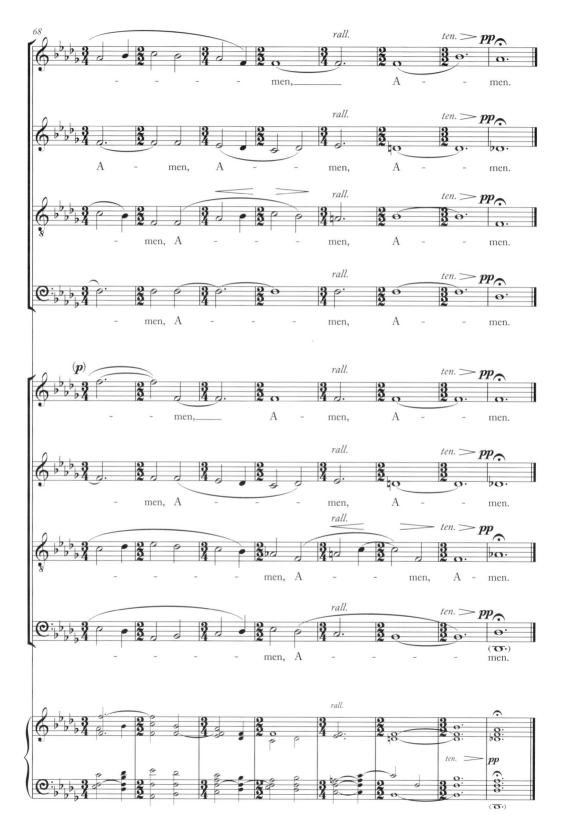

# The heavens are telling

from *The Creation*

Franz Josef Haydn
organ part arr.
Matthew O'Donovan

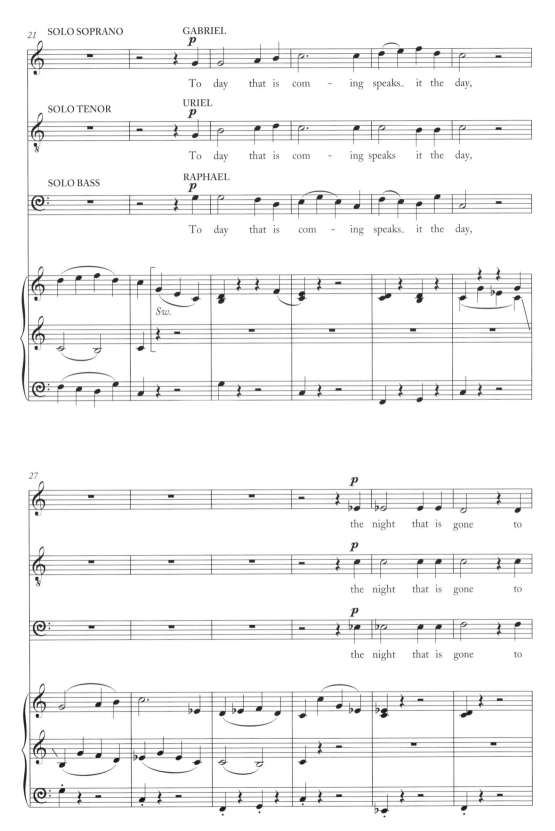

work dis - plays the fir-ma - ment.

-plays, dis - plays the fir-ma - ment.

-plays, dis - plays the fir - ma- ment.

work dis - plays the fir - ma- ment.

Ch. (or Solo) 8'

Sw. 8' 8' 4'

SOLO SOPRANO          GABRIEL

In all the lands re - sounds the word,

SOLO TENOR  URIEL

In all the lands re - sounds the word,

SOLO BASS          RAPHAEL

In all the lands re - sounds the word,

Sw.

-Gt. to Ped. **p** 16'

never un-per-ceiv-ed, ev-er un-der-stood, ev-er, ev-er,

never un-per-ceiv-ed, ev-er un-der-stood, ev-er, ev-er,

never un-per-ceiv-ed, ev-er un-der-stood, ev-er, ev-er,

*Gt. 8' Fl.+Sw.*  *Sw.*  *Gt.*  *Sw.*  *Gt.*

ev - er un - der - stood.

ev - er un - der - stood.

ev - er un - der - stood.

*Sw.*

* see introduction

*Written for the Choir of King's College, Cambridge*

# Vox dicentis, clama

Isaiah 15: 6-11

Edward W. Naylor

63

mon - tem ex - cel - sum a - scen - de tu, a -
*heights of the moun - tains as - scend - ing now, as -*

qui e - van - ge - li - zas Si - on, e - van - ge - li - zas Si - on, a -
*give this mes-sage un-to Zi - on, this mes-sage un-to Zi - on, to*

-cel - sum a-scen-de tu, su - per mon-tem,
*moun-tains as-cend-ing now, give this mes - sage,*

-al - ta, vo - cem tu - am, Su-per
*up thy voice with strength,_____ Up the*

-al - ta vo - cem tu - am, in_____ for-ti-tu-di-
*up thy voice with strength, with strength,_____ be thou not a-*

ex - al - ta vo - cem,
*lift up thy voice,_____*

ex - al - ta vo - cem,
*lift up thy voice,_____*

26 March 1911

# Hear my prayer, O Lord

Psalm 102: 1

Henry Purcell
Ed. H. Watkins Shaw

156

20
cresc. poco a poco
thee, hear my pray-er, O
p cresc. poco a poco
hear my pray-er, O Lord,
cresc. poco a poco
cry - ing come un - to thee, hear my
cresc. poco a poco
-to thee, and let my cry - ing come un - to thee,
cresc. poco a poco
pray-er, O Lord, and let my
p cresc. poco a poco
and let my cry - - - ing come un - to thee,
cresc. poco a poco
and let my
cresc. poco a poco
Lord, and let my cry - ing come un - to thee,

**Source**

This noble fragment, the opening section of an unfinished work, survives only in Fitzwilliam Museum MS 88, one of Purcell's holograph albums, where a blank space is left for its completion. It was composed before 10 Setember 1682.

**Editorial Procedure**

Original key signature was two flats. Marks of style and expression are editorial. The composer having used up all the staves on his page for the voice parts, there is no organ bass in the source. It is right, however, to conceive the anthem as intended to be accompanied, even though the voices disclose a complete harmonic texture.

Grateful acknowledgement is made to the Syndics of the Fitzwilliam Museum for permission to publish from Fitzwilliam MS 88.

*W.S. 1967*

# Remember not, Lord, our offences

Book of Common Prayer, 1662

Henry Purcell
Ed. Walter Emery

# Thou knowest, Lord, the secrets of our hearts

Book of Common Prayer, 1662

Henry Purcell
Ed. H. Watkins Shaw

shut not thy mer-ci-ful ears un - to our pray - er; but spare us,

shut not thy mer-ci-ful ears un - to our pray - er; but spare us,

shut not thy mer-ci-ful ears un - to our pray - er; but spare us,

shut not thy mer-ci-ful ears un - to our pray - er; but spare us,

Lord, spare us, Lord most ho - ly, O God, O God most

Lord, spare us, Lord most ho - ly, O God, O God most

Lord, spare us, Lord most ho - ly, O God, O God most

Lord, spare us, Lord most ho - ly, O God, O God most

# Rejoice in the Lord alway

Philippians 4: 4, 6 & 7

George Rathbone

peace of God, which pass - eth all un - der - stand - ing, shall keep your hearts and

minds through Je - sus Christ our Lord. And the peace of God, which pass - eth all un - der-

ALTO *pp*

And the peace of God, which pass - eth all un - der-

TENOR *pp*

And the peace of God, which pass - eth all un - der-

BASS *pp*

And the peace of God, which pass - eth all un - der-

*Voices only*

poco rit.    a tempo

-stand - ing, shall keep your hearts and minds through Je - sus Christ our Lord.

poco rit.    a tempo

-stand - ing, shall keep your hearts and minds through Je - sus Christ our Lord.

poco rit.    a tempo

-stand - ing, shall keep your hearts and minds through Je - sus Christ our Lord.

poco rit.    a tempo

-stand - ing, shall keep your hearts and minds through Je - sus Christ our Lord.

*mf* Gt.

# I saw the Lord

Isaiah 6: 1-4

John Stainer

high and lift-ed up, high and lift-ed up, and His train fill-ed the tem -

high and lift-ed up, high and lift - ed up, and His train fill-ed the tem -

high and lift-ed up, high and lift - ed up, and His train fill - ed the tem -

high and lift-ed up, high and lift - ed up, and His train fill - ed the tem -

high and lift-ed up, high and lift - ed up.

high and lift-ed up, high and lift - ed up.

high and lift-ed up, high and lift - ed up.

high and lift-ed up, high and lift - ed up.

Ho - ly, Ho - ly, Ho - ly is the Lord of Hosts.

190

O Tri - ni - ty! O U - ni - ty! Be pre - sent as we wor - ship Thee, And

with the songs that an - gels sing, U - nite the hymns of praise___ we

# Ascribe unto the Lord

Psalm 96: 7-10, 2, 3 & 5;
115: 4-8; 8: 13-15

Samuel Sebastian Wesley

*8' coupled to Sw.*

216

feet have they, and walk not: nei - ther speak____ they through their

throat, nei - ther speak____ they through their throat.

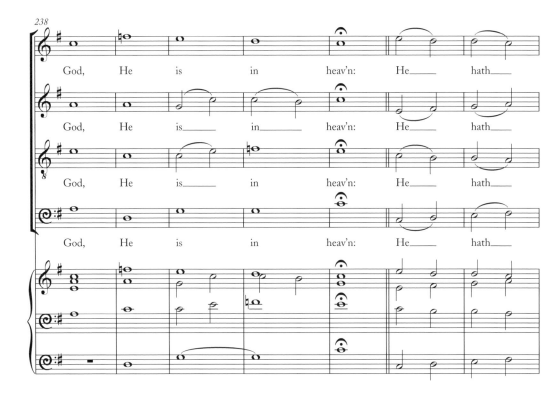

228

# Blessed be the God and Father

1 Peter 1: 3-5, 15-17, 22-25

Samuel Sebastian Wesley

live - ly hope by the re - sur - rec-tion of Je-sus Christ from the dead,

live - ly hope by the re - sur - rec-tion of Je-sus Christ from the dead,

live - ly hope by the re - sur - rec-tion of Je-sus Christ from____ the dead,

live - ly hope by the re - sur - rec-tion of Je-sus Christ from the dead,

*L'istesso tempo*

ALTO *(Unison)*, TENOR and BASS

To an in - he - ri - tance in - cor - rup - ti-ble and un - de - fi - led, that

fad - eth not a - way, re - serv - ed in heaven for you, Who are kept by the

pow - er of God,  through faith  un-to  sal - va - tion  rea-dy  to be  re - veal - ed  in the

**DEC. SOPRANO SOLO**

last  time.  But  as

He  which hath  call - ed you is  ho - ly,  so  be__ ye  ho - ly  in all

man ner  of__ con - ver - sa - tion.  Pass  the time  of your  so - journ-ing  here  in

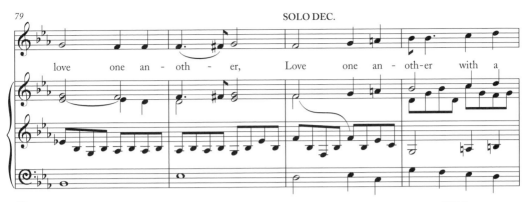

love one an - oth - er, Love one an - oth-er with a

**SOLO DEC.**

pure heart fer - vent-ly, a pure

**CAN. SOPRANOS**

heart____ fer - vent-ly, See that ye love one an -

**SOLO DEC.**

-oth - er, See that ye love,___ that ye love___ one an -

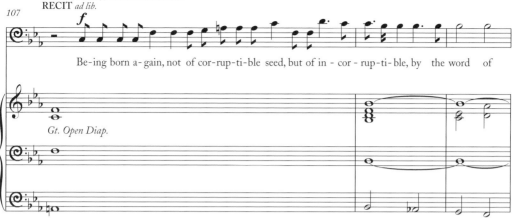

ALTO *(Unison)*, TENOR and BASS
RECIT *ad lib.*

Being born a-gain, not of cor-rup-ti-ble seed, but of in-cor-rup-ti-ble, by the word of

Gt. Open Diap.

add 16'

God. For all flesh is as grass, and all the glo-ry of man as the flow-er of grass. The

Sw. Reed

grass with-er-eth, and the flow-er___ there-of fall - eth a - way.

Clarabella

Sw. Reed

*f* Full Org.

244

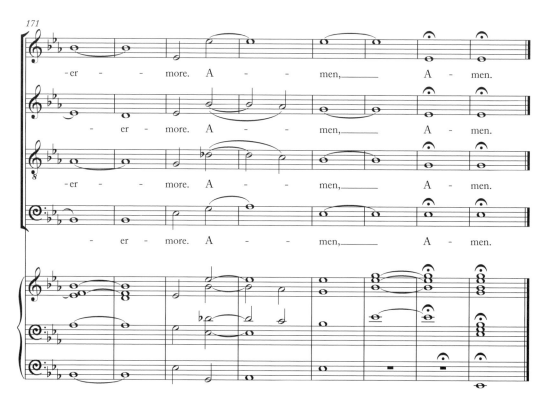